WDB

Why Animals Live in Hives

By Valerie J. Weber

Reading consultant:

Susan Nations, M.Ed., *author/literacy coach/consultant in literacy development*

Science and curriculum consultant:

Debra Voege, M.A., *science curriculum resource teacher*

WEEKLY READER®
PUBLISHING

Please visit our web site at www.garethstevens.com.
For a free color catalog describing our list of high-quality books, call 1-800-542-2595 (USA)
or 1-800-387-3178 (Canada). Our fax: 1-877-542-2596

Library of Congress Cataloging-in-Publication Data
Weber, Valerie.
　　Why animals live in hives.
　　　　p. cm.—(Where animals live)
　　Includes bibliographical references and index.
　　ISBN-10: 0-8368-8795-6　ISBN-13: 978-0-8368-8795-2 (lib. bdg.)
　　ISBN-10: 0-8368-8802-2　ISBN-13: 978-0-8368-8802-7 (softcover)
　　1. Honeybee—Juvenile literature.　2. Beehives—Juvenile literature.
I. Title.
QL568.A6 W
595.79'9—dc22   2007028185

This edition first published in 2008 by
Weekly Reader® Books
An Imprint of Gareth Stevens Publishing
1 Reader's Digest Road
Pleasantville, NY 10570-7000　USA

Senior Managing Editor: Lisa M. Guidone
Senior Editor: Barbara Bakowski
Creative Director: Lisa Donovan
Senior Designer: Keith Plechaty
Production Designer: Amy Ray, *Studio Montage*
Photo Researcher: Diane Laska-Swanke

Photo Credits: Cover © Digital Vision/Getty Images; pp. 1, 3, 4, 6, 9, 12, 17 © Photodisc/Don Farrall/Getty Images;
p. 5 © Juniors Bildarchiv/Alamy; p. 7 © isifa Image Service s.r.o./Alamy; pp. 8, 16 © E. S. Ross/Visuals Unlimited;
pp. 10, 18 © Stephen McDaniel; p. 11 © Dr. Jeremy Burgess/Photo Researchers, Inc.; p. 13 © Premaphotos/naturepl.
com; p. 14 © Kim Taylor/naturepl.com; p. 15 © John B. Free/naturepl.com; p. 19 © Pete Oxford/naturepl.com; p. 20
© Nick Greaves/Alamy; p. 21 © Bill Beatty/Visuals Unlimited

Printed in the United States of America

1 2 3 4 5 6 7 8 9 10 09 08 07

Table of Contents

Chapter 1 Home in the Hive. 4

Chapter 2 Building the Hive. 6

Chapter 3 One Home, Many Jobs. 9

Chapter 4 Cupboards and Nurseries. 12

Chapter 5 Keeping the Hive Safe and Sound. 17

Glossary. 22

To Find Out More. 23

Index 24

Words that appear in the glossary are
printed in **boldface** type the first time
they occur in the text.

Chapter 1

Home in the Hive

Have you ever seen honeybees buzzing in a field of wildflowers? Did you wonder what the bees are doing? Where do they go when they are done?

Like people at a grocery store, the bees are collecting food. Like the shoppers, the bees are going to take their food home.

Honeybees make their home in a hive. There, bees store their food, raise their young, and sleep. In the hive, they stay dry when rain falls and warm when the weather turns cold. The bees also stay safe from animals that want to eat them or their honey.

Thousands of honeybees live in a single hive.

Chapter 2

Building the Hive

Honeybees build their hive from wax that they create in their bodies. Each honeybee joins its tiny wax flakes with those from other honeybees. Bees use more than 2 pounds (1 kilogram) of wax to make a hive. They work from the top and build downward. Using their **mouthparts**, they make tiny rooms. Each room is called a **cell**.

Hundreds of cells make up a large hive. Each cell has six sides. The six-sided shape has more space to hold honey and takes less wax to build than any other shape.

A hive is made up of many six-sided cells.

cells

Each level of cells in a hive has a different purpose. In most hives, bees store honey in the upper cells. In the middle cells, bees keep **pollen** that they collect from flowers. The eggs and young bees live in a **brood nest**, or nursery, in the lower cells.

A hive can store about 40 pounds (18 kg) of honey.

honey

pollen

Chapter 3

One Home, Many Jobs

A beehive is a buzz of activity. It is home to three different kinds of bees. Thousands of female **worker bees** and male **drones** live in the hive. Each hive has only one **queen**, though. The queen is a bit larger than the other bees. She lays tiny eggs in huge numbers. She often produces more than 1,500 eggs each day. The eggs are so small that together they weigh as much as one queen bee!

Drones live only to **mate** with the queen so she can lay eggs. Soon after drones do their job, they die.

Worker bees feed the queen. They produce her food in **glands**, or special body parts, on their heads.

Each kind of bee has a different task in the hive.

queen

worker

drone

3 1833 05464 4510

Worker bees have other important jobs, too. They work both outside and inside the hive. Worker bees often fly 2 to 3 miles (3 to 5 kilometers) from the hive to gather **nectar** from flowers. Nectar is a sweet liquid made by flowers. The bees will turn the nectar into honey.

In one trip, a worker bee visits fifty to one hundred flowers.

Chapter 4

Cupboards and Nurseries

The bees spit the nectar into a cell. Once the nectar turns to honey, the worker bees use wax to close off the cell. When the workers need food, they open the cell, just as a person opens a kitchen cupboard. The bees in one hive can make and store about 2 pounds (1 kg) of honey a day.

The workers even pack up honey and take it on their trips out of the hive. It's a picnic for bees!

On these trips, worker bees also collect pollen from flowers. They store the pollen in the cells to eat later.

A worker bee collects pollen from flowers. The bee carries the pollen in "baskets" on its back legs.

pollen

larvae

When bee eggs hatch in the hive's nursery, **larvae** come out. Each of the larvae looks like a white worm curled inside its cell. Most of the larvae become worker bees.

Larvae live in a part of the hive called the brood nest.

Workers have a lot to do! They must feed the hundreds of larvae many times every day. Most hives hold from eight thousand to eighty thousand worker bees to do the job.

Larvae grow quickly by eating the food workers bring.

When the larvae reach their full size, worker bees seal off the cells. The larvae become **pupae**, which slowly turn into adult bees. The bees then chew their way out of the cells.

In about two weeks, pupae grow into adult bees.

Chapter 5

Keeping the Hive Safe and Sound

Worker bees defend their hive. Some bees stand guard at the entrance. **Predators**, such as bears and other animals, are after the bees' honey. The bees find safety in numbers. They will sting any intruder. No predator wants to risk being stung by hundreds of bees!

Does your home ever get too hot? The bees' home becomes too hot sometimes. If the bees' eggs get too warm, they will not hatch. Bees do not need air-conditioning to cool their home, though. Worker bees cool the hive by beating their wings very quickly.

Bees cool the hive by fanning their wings.

When the air is cold, worker bees gather around the nursery. Their bodies give off enough heat to keep the eggs warm.

Worker bees huddle close to keep the brood nest warm.

Sometimes, a human family outgrows its home, and the family moves to a new home. A beehive can become too crowded, too! When that happens, the bees need to move to a new home.

When the queen leaves a hive, thousands of workers follow her.

When the hive is full of bees, the queen flies away. Worker bees fill their stomachs with food from the hive. Then they join the queen. They all follow **scout bees** that lead them to a new home near flowers. There, they build a new hive.

Honeybees often build their hives in hollow trees.

Glossary

brood nest: the area in the hive where the young are cared for

cell: a small, six-sided space in a hive

drones: male bees that have no sting and do not gather honey

glands: parts of the body that make certain substances and release them to the rest of the body

larvae: insects in the very young, wingless stage, which look like worms

mate: to come together to make eggs or babies

mouthparts: body parts near the mouth of an insect that are used to gather or eat food

nectar: a sweet liquid produced by some plants

pollen: a fine dust produced by plants that helps them make seeds

predators: animals that hunt or kill for food

pupae: insects in a middle stage between larvae and adults

queen: female honeybee that lays eggs

scout bees: bees that explore an area to get information about it

worker bees: female bees that gather food and take care of the hive, eggs, and larvae

To Find Out More

Books

Bee. Watch It Grow (series). Barrie Watts (Smart Apple Media)

Bees and Their Hives. Animal Homes (series). Linda Tagliaferro (Capstone Press)

Busy, Buzzy Bees. Rookie Read-About Science (series). Allan Fowler (Capstone Press)

Honey Bees and Hives. Lola M. Schaefer (Capstone Press)

The Magic School Bus Inside a Beehive. Joanna Cole (Scholastic)

Web Sites

Kidport Reference Library
www.kidport.com/RefLIb/Science/AnimalHomes/Hives.htm
Find out about social insects that live in hives.

Nature: Alien Empire
www.pbs.org/wnet/nature/alienempire/multimedia/hive.html
Enter the bees' hive and learn more about building and living in a hive.

Publisher's note to educators and parents: Our editors have carefully reviewed these web sites to ensure that they are suitable for children. Many web sites change frequently, however, and we cannot guarantee that a site's future contents will continue to meet our high standards of quality and educational value. Be advised that children should be closely supervised whenever they access the Internet.

Index

brood nest 8, 14, 19

cell 6–8, 12, 13, 14, 16

drone 9–10

eggs 8, 9, 10, 14, 18–19

flowers 4, 8, 11, 13, 21

hatching 14, 18

honey 5, 8, 11, 12–13, 17

larvae 14–16

mating 10

mouthparts 6

nectar 11, 12

pollen 8, 13

predators 5, 17

pupae 16

queen 9–10, 20–21

scout bee 21

wax 6–7, 12

worker bee 9, 10–16, 17–21

About the Author

A writer and editor for more than twenty-five years, Valerie Weber especially loves working in children's publishing. Her book topics have been endlessly engaging— from the weird wonders of the sea, to the lives of girls during World War II, to the making of movies. She is grateful to her family, including her husband and daughters, and her friends for offering their support and for listening to the odd facts she has discovered during her work. Did you know, for example, that frogs use their eyeballs to push food down into their stomachs?